...STERS!

Alison Hawes

Story illustrated by
Ned Woodman

In this story

 Tim

 The Pest

 Big Biffo

 The Ice Monster

Tricky words

- film
- monster
- laughed
- watch
- toilet
- screamed

Introduce these tricky words and help the reader when they come across them later!

Story starter

Tim lives with his mum and his little sister. His mum is always making him look after his sister. Tim calls her the Pest. One day, Tim wanted to see a film called *The Ice Monster*.

Tim, the Pest and the Ice Monster

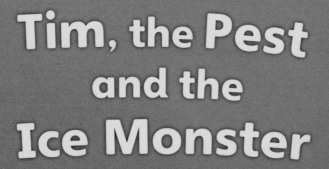

Tim wanted to see a film.
The film was called
The Ice Monster.

But the Pest wanted to go and see the film, too.

Big Biffo saw Tim with the Pest.

He laughed at Tim.

Why did Big Biffo laugh at Tim?

Tim wanted to go in and
watch the film, but the Pest
wanted to go to the toilet.

Big Biffo laughed at Tim.

Tim wanted to watch the film, but the Pest wanted an ice lolly.

Big Biffo laughed and laughed at Tim.

In the film, the Ice Monster put his ice hands on a boy's neck.

The boy in the film screamed.

The Pest put her ice lolly on Big Biffo's neck.

Big Biffo screamed.

Tim and the Pest laughed and laughed!

Why did Big Biffo scream?

Text Detective

- What did the Pest want to do during the film?
- Why did the Pest put her ice lolly on Big Biffo's neck?

Word Detective

- **Phonic Focus:** Final letter sounds
  Page 5: Find a word that ends with 'th'.
- Page 6: Find a word that means 'look at'.
- Page 6: Find the word 'wanted' twice.

Super Speller

Read these words:

her   his   saw

Now try to spell them!

HA! HA! HA!

Q What do dogs eat when they go to watch a film?

A Pup-corn!

Before Reading

Find out about

- How monsters in films are made to look scary

Tricky words

- film
- monster
- scary
- ape
- model

Introduce these tricky words and help the reader when they come across them later!

Text starter

Monsters in films look scary but how are they made to look scary? Sometimes they are models, sometimes it is make-up and sometimes the monsters are made on a computer.

Monsters on Film

Monsters in films look scary!
In the film *King Kong*,
King Kong is a monster ape.

King Kong looks scary in the film, but it is just a model of a monster!

The model of King Kong was only 60cm tall!

In the film *Frankenstein*,
a man called Frankenstein
makes a scary monster.

In films, monsters look scary, but it is just make-up!

In the film *Jaws*,
Jaws is a monster shark.

In the film, Jaws looks scary, but it is just a model of a shark!

In the film *Jurassic Park*, the scary monsters are dinosaurs.

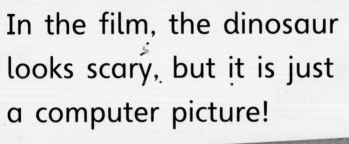

In the film, the dinosaur looks scary, but it is just a computer picture!

So are monsters in films scary?

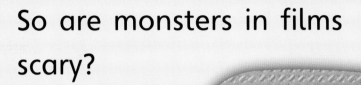
make-up

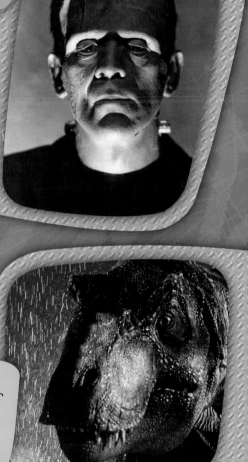

model

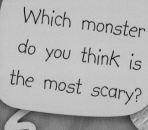
Which monster do you think is the most scary?

computer picture

Quiz

Text Detective

- Is Jaws a real shark?
- Have you ever been scared by a monster in a film?

Word Detective

- **Phonic Focus:** Final letter sounds
  Page 16: Find a word that ends with 'm'.
- Page 15: Find a word that means 'frightening'.
- Page 16: Find a word that rhymes with 'books'.

Super Speller

Read these words:

makes   are   just

Now try to spell them!

HA! HA! HA!

Q What do you do if King Kong sits in front of you at the cinema?

A Miss most of the film!

24